Benjamin Franklin

Genius Inventor and Electricity Pioneer

Peggy Parks

THOMSON
———
GALE

San Diego • Detroit • New York • San Francisco • Cleveland
New Haven, Conn. • Waterville, Maine • London • Munich

THOMSON

★ ™

GALE

For more information, contact
The Gale Group, Inc.
27500 Drake Rd.
Farmington Hills, MI 48331-3535
Or you can visit our Internet site at http://www.gale.com

Photo Credits: page 1 © Adobe Stock Photography; page 27 © American Philosophical Society; pages 5, 6-7, 8, 9, 12-13, 14, 15, 20, 21, 23, 25, 36, 42, 45, 54, 60 © Corbis; pages 11, 24 © Corel; pages 35, 41, 41 (inset), 57 Courtesy The Franklin Institute Online; page 29 Courtesy of the Library Company of Philadelphia; pages 10, 17, 23, 26, 30, 37, 50, 56 Courtesy The Library of Congress; page 52 Courtesy of NOAA; pages 19, 49 © North Wind Picture Archives; cover, page 1 © Pennsylvania Academy of the Fine Arts; pages 33, 38 © PhotoDisc; page 46 Courtesy of The Theodore Presser Foundation

LIBRARY OF CONGRESS CATALOGING-IN-PUBLICATION DATA

Parks, Peggy J., 1951-
    Benjamin Franklin / by Peggy Parks.
       p. cm. — (Giants of science series)
    Includes index.
    Summary: Surveys the life and accomplishments of American author, printer, scientist, inventor, community leader, and diplomat, Benjamin Franklin.
    ISBN 1-56711-658-2 (alk. paper)
    1. Franklin, Benjamin, 1706-1790—Juvenile literature. 2. Scientists—United States—Biography—Juvenile literature. 3. Inventors—United States—Biography—Juvenile literature. [1. Franklin, Benjamin, 1706-1790. 2. Statesmen. 3. Scientists. 4. Inventors. 5. Printers.]   I. Title. II. Series: Giants of science.
    Q143.F8P38 2003
    509.2—dc21
    [B]   2002007247

Printed in China
10 9 8 7 6 5 4 3 2 1

CONTENTS

An Electrifying Experiment

In June 1752, a retired Philadelphia printer named Benjamin Franklin set out to prove a theory he had about electricity. Long fascinated with thunderstorms, Franklin believed that lightning was a form of electricity. If this were true, he reasoned, then lightning must be a natural electrical current that existed within clouds.

Benjamin Franklin was "one of the most illustrious... thinkers on earth."

What he needed was a way to attract lightning to see if it behaved like electricity. He decided that the simplest way to do this was to fly a kite during a storm.

Franklin needed a special kind of kite to make his experiment work: one that could withstand the wind and rain of the storm, and one that was outfitted with metal to attract lightning. He built his own kite with two lightweight strips of cedar, a silk handkerchief, and a sharp pointed wire for the top. To the bottom he attached a length of twine, and then he tied a silk ribbon onto the twine and fastened a key to the ribbon. He was quite sure that once the pointed metal attracted lightning, electricity would then travel through the conductor (the wet twine) and electrify the key. His kite was complete. All he needed was a thunderstorm. Eventually, a storm rolled in.

Opposite: *Benjamin Franklin proved his theory that lightning was a form of electricity.*

Early scientists discovered they could produce electricity by creating friction.

Franklin, accompanied by his son William, took the kite and walked to a nearby field, where he stood in the open doorway of a shed. He held the end of the twine so the key dangled near his hand, and he raised his kite. After he had waited for quite a long time and watched several dark thunderclouds pass overhead, he began to grow discouraged. Then he noticed something: Loose fibers of the rain-soaked twine stood straight out as if suspended in midair—which he

knew meant that the fibers were electrified. Next came the real test. Franklin touched his knuckle to the key and felt a sharp electrical shock. He had proven his theory: Lightning and electricity were indeed one and the same.

Early Electrical Studies

Because of his famous kite experiment, people sometimes believe that Benjamin Franklin discovered electricity, but that is not true. Greek philosophers had studied electrical properties as far back as 600 B.C. They observed that when amber (a translucent fossil) was rubbed, lightweight objects would stick to it. Other philosophers continued this research, and in 300 B.C., they found that the same experiment worked with different types of matter besides amber.

Nearly 2,000 years passed before electrical research uncovered any new findings. Then, during the 1600s and early 1700s, European scientists developed a renewed interest in this mysterious phenomenon called electricity, whose name was derived from "electrums," the Latin word for amber.

By the 1740s, scientists had determined that electrical forces existed naturally in the form of static electricity, which was created through friction when a substance was rubbed. These scientists identified two types of electricity: vitreous, produced on glass that was

When amber is rubbed, objects will stick to it.

rubbed with silk; and resinous, produced when resin (an organic substance like amber or tar) was rubbed with wool or fur. They built and experimented with friction machines, which were glass jars mounted on a wooden frame with a handle on the side. When the handle was turned, it caused material inside to rub against the glass and create static electricity.

These discoveries were advanced for the times; still, knowledge about electricity remained inconclusive and fuzzy. Scientists knew that electricity existed naturally but they still wondered why it existed and where it came from. A few suspected electricity's connection with lightning, but most were skeptical about it. Instead, they believed lightning was caused by poisonous gases that exploded in the air. Electricity remained a strange, mysterious force that amazed people but could not be explained. Some were even frightened by it, and thought it was a form of magic.

A Scientific Breakthrough

Scientists were especially puzzled by the fact that they could produce electricity with friction, but they could not collect and hold it in any sort of container. That changed in 1746, when a Dutch scientist named Pieter van Musschenbroek invented the Leyden jar, an apparatus that proved to be a significant breakthrough in electrical research. The Leyden jar consisted of a glass vial partially filled with water, a thick wire through which an electrical

"The electrical fluid is attracted by points. We do not know whether this is a property of lightning. But since they agree in all particulars wherein we can already compare them, is it not probable that they agree likewise in this? Let the experiment be made."

—BENJAMIN FRANKLIN, FROM HIS NOTES ON EXPERIMENTS

charge could travel, and a cork that sealed the vial shut. The wire rested in the water and protruded through the cork; when it was exposed to friction, electricity was produced and stored in the jar. Because it could store electricity, the Leyden jar was the first known condenser.

In the world of science, the Leyden jar was considered an important invention—one that particularly fascinated Benjamin Franklin and intensified his interest in electricity. He believed more than ever that lightning and electricity were identical, and he was determined to prove it. With his famous kite experiment he did exactly that. No longer would scientists wonder where electricity came from, or view it as something baffling or unexplainable. Even though people before him may have suspected electricity's connection with lightning, Franklin was the first to prove it.

The Leyden jar was the first container used to store electricity.

Electricity had fascinated Franklin for much of his life, but he was also interested in everything related to science. He had a keen, inquisitive mind and was never satisfied just to know about natural phenomena—he had to know why natural phenomena occurred. His countless discoveries had a profound impact on the world of science and his long list of inventions included the electrical battery, lightning rods, the Franklin stove, bifocals, and swim fins.

Although he observed nature and made scientific discoveries nearly his entire life, Franklin conducted his most famous studies and experiments after he had become a successful and wealthy printer in Philadelphia. The story of this man—who became known as one of the most brilliant scientists of all time—began in Boston, the town where he was born.

Boston Beginnings

Benjamin Franklin was born on January 17, 1706. He was the eighth child of Josiah and Abiah Franklin, and the fifteenth child of Josiah, whose first wife had died in childbirth. At the time of Benjamin's birth, America was a relatively new settlement, less than 100 years old and composed of 13 colonies under British rule. The seaport

This bust marks Benjamin Franklin's birthplace, on which a more modern building was constructed.

Josiah Franklin left Northamptonshire, England, in 1683.

town of Boston was part of one of the oldest settlements in America, the Massachusetts Bay Colony.

Josiah Franklin had emigrated from England to America in 1683. His family lived in the region of Northamptonshire for more than 300 years, and like many English subjects, Josiah had always been loyal to his native country. His religious beliefs, though, were different from the traditional teachings advocated by the Church of England, and dissension was not tolerated. In fact, the church had begun to persecute people who did not adhere to its religious teachings. So, like thousands of other English subjects who sought religious and personal freedom, Josiah left England to make a fresh start in America.

After he settled with his family in Boston, Josiah became a chandler, a person who made candles and soap. He was considered a hard worker and an intelligent man who possessed integrity as well as common sense. These characteristics had a positive influence on his son Benjamin, who later wrote that his father was so well respected that he was often consulted by neighbors and others in the community for his good judgment and sound advice.

Benjamin was raised in a household full of children—sometimes as many as 13 were seated at the dinner table—so he learned at an early age how to get along with others. He was an outgoing,

11

social boy who was a leader among his peers, and he was filled with natural curiosity and a sense of adventure. Because of his home's proximity to the Atlantic shore, he was always drawn to the sea and constantly watched ships as they came and went. He could only imagine the exotic places they visited in other parts of the world. He believed that someday he, too, would see those places.

Short-Lived Schooling

As a child, Benjamin had little formal schooling. His father intended for him to enter the ministry, and he enrolled his son in the town's grammar school when the boy was eight years old. Benjamin excelled and quickly went to the head of his class.

One year later, Josiah reconsidered his son's future and decided that he should focus on a trade rather than the ministry. He sent Benjamin to a different school, where a local schoolmaster taught the children of tradesmen. Benjamin did well at grammar and writing but failed mathematics, so after less than a year his father withdrew him. Benjamin's school years were over. At the age of ten, he went to work in his father's shop, where he cut wicks for candles, filled molds, helped customers, and ran errands.

Benjamin Franklin dreamed of adventure at sea.

Young Tradesman

Although Benjamin's formal education had ended after less than two years, he continued to learn from his father and showed high intelligence from a young age. His natural curiosity and thirst for knowledge made him an avid reader, and he read any books that were available to him.

By the time Benjamin was 12 years old, he had grown tired of the chandlery trade, which he found dull and tedious. Josiah knew that his son loved the water and feared he would run off to sea, so he considered other job options for Benjamin. He spoke with his son James, who was nine years older than Benjamin and owned a printing business in Boston. James needed a helper to work in his shop, so he and Josiah decided that Benjamin would go to work for him.

From the beginning, Benjamin excelled at his job. He easily handled the physical challenges of work in the printing shop, where he moved heavy sets of lead type and ran manual printing presses. Also, because he was such a good reader and had a natural talent for language, he soon became a proficient editor and proofreader. Within a short time, James decided to make Benjamin his apprentice, a kind of student-in-training for the printing trade. This legally bound Benjamin to work for his brother for the next nine years.

A Hunger for Knowledge

Benjamin worked in his brother's printing shop six days a week and spent the rest of his time reading. He read before work in

Benjamin became his older brother James's apprentice at the family printing press.

the morning and late into the night. He borrowed and read his father's books and bought many of his own, which he read and then sold to buy more books. He read not just for enjoyment, but to increase his knowledge about the world. He taught himself science, mathematics, navigation, grammar, and logic, as well as a variety of other subjects.

Because Benjamin was so curious about the world outside of Boston, he hungered to learn geography. He used his family's morning and evening prayer sessions (when he was supposed to learn about religion) to teach himself geography from four large maps that hung on the walls of his home.

Early Discoveries

It was during his boyhood that Benjamin tried his earliest known experiments, one of which used the power of wind. On a windy summer day, as he flew a kite on the bank of a pond, he decided to take a swim. He did not want to stop flying his kite, so he floated on the pond's surface, held his kite in one hand, and flew it above him. Before long, he felt the wind tugging him across the water. He had discovered a way to swim without any effort. As he lay on his back and surrendered to the wind's power, he was delighted to let his "sail kite" pull him from one side of the pond to the other.

Another of Benjamin's early experiments also involved swimming. He made what he called "hand palettes," oval-shaped paddles that he held in his hands, and wooden flippers for his feet, which he thought would mimic a fish's tail. The hand paddles did

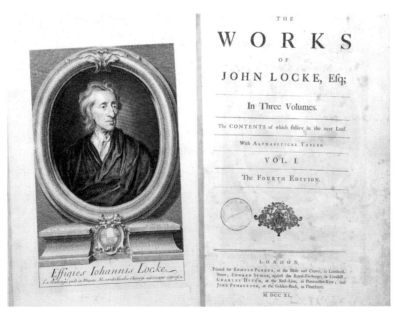

Benjamin Franklin's avid reading included the works of English philosopher John Locke.

increase his speed in the water, but they quickly tired his wrists. Also, the flippers were stiff and heavy, so they did not propel him through the water as he had hoped. Yet even though Benjamin was not quite satisfied with his swimming apparatuses, the crude flippers he invented were actually the first known swim fins.

A Controversial Newspaper

When Benjamin was 15, his brother James began to publish a newspaper called the *New England Courant*. James vowed that his paper would not be like most papers, which were biased in favor of the establishment (government). Instead, the *Courant* would represent freedom of thought and would be lively and full of independent opinions—even those that directly challenged the establishment.

From the very beginning, the *Courant* became known as irreverent and was publicly denounced by influential people such as Cotton Mather, a prominent Puritan minister and writer. Mather, who spoke out in favor of inoculations for diseases like smallpox, was enraged when James defied him and printed the viewpoint of someone who disagreed with Mather. In response, Mather called the *Courant* a "notorious, scandalous paper" and referred to "the wicked printer and his accomplices who every week publish a vile paper to lessen and blacken the ministers of the town."

Mather's hot protests against the *Courant* did not dissuade James; if anything, he became more determined than ever to keep the newspaper bold and outspoken. Benjamin enjoyed the controversy and wanted to contribute his own written opinions, but he knew his brother would not print anything he wrote. So the mischievous young man thought of a way to get involved: He invented a fictitious person named "Silence Dogood," and wrote controversial letters to the paper in her name. Benjamin disguised his handwriting so James would not suspect the truth, and then slipped the letters under the print shop door late at night.

Silence's—or rather, Benjamin's—letters freely poked fun at various people and events, and were especially critical of Harvard College (the college Cotton Mather had attended), which Silence said was snobbish, and catered only to the rich. The letters also spoke out against a number of injustices in the world, such as the unfair treatment of women and girls.

James Franklin's newspaper, the New England Courant, *was denounced by Cotton Mather, an influentiual Puritan minister, for its anti-establishment ideas.*

The quality of the writing, as well as the depth of information included in the letters, made everyone believe they were real—which delighted Benjamin. James undoubtedly knew that "Silence Dogood" was a fictitious name, yet no one suspected that the letters were actually written by Benjamin.

The Turning Point

The disrespectful tone of the *New England Courant* and the outrage it caused among influential people made the authorities angry and watchful. Thus, when James printed a fictitious letter that criticized the authorities' handling of a crime, he was arrested for contempt and sent to a Boston jail. This left Benjamin in charge of the *Courant*, and he was pleased and even a bit boastful as he accepted management responsibilities for the newspaper.

After one month in jail, James was released. Before long, however, he was ordered to stop publication of the *Courant* because it was

viewed as mocking and disrespectful of religion, as well as the establishment in general. To get around this order, he began to publish the
newspaper in Benjamin's name, instead of his own.

The following seven months were a tumultuous time for the
Franklin brothers. Benjamin admitted that he had written the
Silence Dogood letters, and because James had been fooled—and
was jealous of his brother's cleverness—he was infuriated.
Benjamin also had a feisty, independent spirit that often provoked
James, and the two clashed regularly. They disagreed about almost
everything, and James frequently lost his temper and beat
Benjamin.

By 1723 the situation had grown
much worse, and Benjamin knew he
could no longer work for James, even
if it meant he had to break their
apprenticeship agreement. James
suspected that Benjamin was about
to break their agreement, and to
retaliate, he spoke with his fellow
printers to ensure that no one would
hire Benjamin. This presented
Benjamin with a problem. With no
employment available, what would
he do? Even though he was only 17 years old, he felt he had no
choice but to leave Boston—the city where was born, and where he
had always lived. He would move to New York, find a job, and start
a new life.

"A life as full as Franklin's
could not be captured in a
phrase—or a volume."

— H.W. BRANDS, BIOGRAPHER

A New Beginning

Franklin sold some of his books to earn money for his trip, then he
boarded a ship and arrived in New York three days later. He expected to find an abundance of available jobs in the bustling city.
Instead, he found that New York did not have any newspapers, and
the city's only printer, William Bradford, did not need any helpers.
Franklin did learn from Bradford that his son, who lived in
Philadelphia, might need a printing apprentice. With no other
options, and very little money in his pocket, Franklin set off for
another new city.

Life in Philadelphia

When Franklin arrived in Philadelphia, he learned that Bradford's son had already hired an apprentice, but he was able to find work with another printer named Samuel Keimer. Over the following months, he proved himself to be a skilled and talented worker, and he became indispensable to his employer's printing business. In time he became well known and earned a reputation as an intelligent young man.

Good printers were scarce in Philadelphia, and those who were good got noticed. Franklin won so much respect in his trade that he caught the attention of Sir William Keith, the governor of Pennsylvania, who praised his talents and urged him to start his own printing business. In fact, Keith was so impressed that he promised Franklin financial help in the form of a letter of credit. Franklin could travel to England and buy the equipment he needed, and the letter would serve as Keith's promise to pay for it. Franklin could not believe his good fortune: He would be able visit a place he had only dreamed about, and he would return home a business owner. Filled with hopes for his future, he booked passage on a ship bound for England. When the ship left port, Keith's letter of credit had still not arrived, but Franklin was not worried. He expected that the letter would be delivered at the last minute with the other mail that would travel aboard the ship, and he would be able to retrieve it in London.

Benjamin Franklin moved to Philadelphia and apprenticed under Samuel Keimer.

Stranded in England

As it turned out, the governor's promise was too good to be true. When the ship arrived in London on Christmas Eve, 1724, Franklin made a shocking discovery: There was no letter of credit for him. The governor, known by his peers as someone who promised much and delivered little, had failed him. Franklin was stranded 3,000 miles away from home, with no job and little money.

Franklin was disheartened, but he was fiercely determined to make the best of his situation. Before long, he was able to find work at a printing house. For the next year and a half, he lived and worked in London. There, he socialized frequently and made many friends. The city was home to many of the world's great intellectuals; and although Franklin did not have opportunities to socialize with these men, he made it a point to meet as many people as he could. One man with whom he became acquainted, Dr. Henry Pemberton, promised to introduce Franklin to Sir Isaac Newton, a mathematical genius who was famous for his laws of motion and theories of light and gravity. Franklin had a deep admiration for Newton and was extremely disappointed when the meeting never happened.

Even though Franklin's arrival in England had started out on a less than positive note, he became comfortable and enjoyed his life there. After he had lived in London for 18 months, however, he found that he missed Philadelphia. So, in July 1726, he boarded a ship and headed home to America.

Benjamin Franklin was disappointed that he did not get the chance to meet Sir Isaac Newton.

Opposite: *Newton's light studies led to his inventing the first reflecting telescope in 1688.*

Scientific Discoveries at Sea

Franklin's long ocean voyage gave him plenty of opportunities to satisfy his inquisitive mind and prove himself to be a budding scientist. On the way back to Philadelphia, he observed fish and other sea life, and he recorded his observations in a journal.

Franklin was so inquisitive about nature that even the simplest forms of plant life caught his attention. He noticed some gulf weed (a form of seaweed) in the water that had been stirred up from a storm, and used a hook to pull a sample aboard. Among the tangled branches he saw clusters of tiny shellfish (which he called "vegetable animals") that clung to the weed and appeared to be growing out of it. He also observed a small crab that was the same color as the seaweed, and he wondered if the vegetable animals grew from the branches and then evolved into crabs. Franklin reasoned that if silkworms and butterflies changed form, then it might also be possible for seaweed to evolve into crabs. To test his theory, he placed some gulf weed without crabs in a bucket of seawater, and left it there to see if crabs would grow. They did not, and after the seaweed died, he realized that his theory had been wrong.

Franklin also became intrigued with "flying fish"—mackerel-like fish with large fins that allowed them to glide a few yards above the

"He was a great scientist, by whatever standards we test him, and he gave to the world of science knowledge of lasting importance and novelty. In any list of great original scientists of the world, Franklin's name must always appear. For fundamental importance, for daring imagination, and for successful endeavor, he must always be ranked with the leaders."

— HOWARD MCCLENAHAN, FORMER DEAN OF PRINCETON UNIVERSITY

Opposite: *Franklin's inquisitive mind, fed by his voracious reading, led him to examine the natural world.*

water so they would not be caught and eaten by dolphins. He observed the dolphins as they raced beneath the flying fish, ready to snap them up as soon as they touched the water. He also studied sharks, which he called the "mortal enemy to swimmers." These fearsome-looking creatures moved around the ship, and Franklin noticed that they were constantly surrounded by schools of smaller pilot fish. He determined that the sharks were not interested in eating the pilot fish, but instead seemed to have some sort of partnership with them: The pilot fish hunted and distinguished prey for the sharks, while the sharks made sure the smaller fish were not gobbled up by dolphins.

Celestial Observations

Franklin not only observed the sea during his voyage, but he also kept a close watch on the sky. One night after a storm, when the moon was full, he saw something unlike anything he had ever seen before: a moonlight rainbow, which was formed by the bright light of the moon shining through raindrops in the air.

Franklin's travels across the Atlantic allowed him to observe sea life. He studied the sharks constantly surrounded by pilot fish.

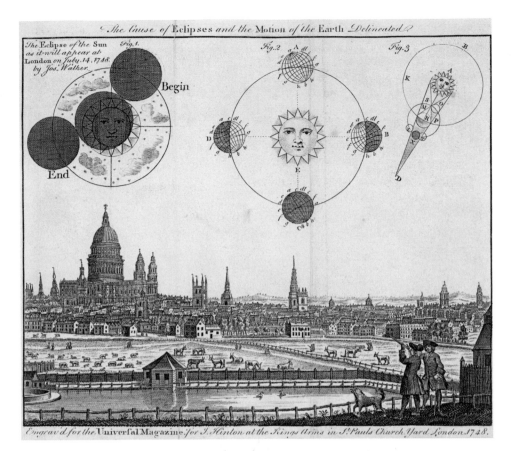

On his journey to England, Franklin witnessed an eclipse of the moon and of the sun. This drawing shows an interpretation of a solar eclipse in the 1700s.

He also witnessed two eclipses, one of the sun and one of the moon. One afternoon while he was on the ship's deck, it suddenly began to grow dark, and Franklin assumed this was an eclipse of the sun. A few weeks later, he stayed up past midnight to observe and time a half-eclipse of the moon. Based on his calculations, he estimated the ship's distance from London and surmised that America could not be far away.

He hoped he was right, because after 12 long weeks at sea, he was extremely eager to be back home again. Each day he began to watch for signs that land might be close. On October 9, 1726, one of the ship's crew yelled the long-awaited words: "LAND! LAND!" Franklin was home at last.

25

Back Home in Philadelphia

Franklin returned to Philadelphia with even more determination and ambition than before. The experience of life as part of a different culture had increased his strength and confidence, and had given him a new level of sophistication. He even benefited from the devastating blow the governor had dealt him because he had learned to rely on himself and his own abilities, rather than on the promises of others.

After several months, he found a job in the printing trade. For the next two years, he worked hard to build his knowledge and skills, and once again he earned a reputation as a talented Philadelphia printer. Yet even as he worked for other people, Franklin never let go of the dream that had sent him to London in the first place: to have his own printing business.

In July 1729, he got his wish. He purchased a newspaper from his former employer, Samuel Keimer, and began to publish his own paper, which he named the *Pennsylvania Gazette*.

Franklin's talent and creativity, as well as his years of work experience, helped him make the *Gazette* a success, and before long it became the leading paper in Pennsylvania. It included articles, letters, and personal opinions, but because Franklin had no desire to end up in trouble like his brother, he was careful not to print items that were overly disrespectful or provocative toward the establishment.

This is the printing press Franklin used.

Family Life

When Franklin first moved to Philadelphia from Boston, he became acquainted with Deborah Read, the daughter of his landlady. He had begun to court her, but then abandoned thoughts of marriage because of his impending journey to England. Now, seven years later, he resumed his courtship of Deborah. On September 1, 1730, Benjamin Franklin and Deborah Read were married in a common law ceremony in Philadelphia, and in 1731, Franklin's son William was born. The Franklin's second son, Francis Folger, was born in 1732.

Poor Richard's Almanack

Less than two years after he began to publish the *Gazette*, Franklin was well on the way toward financial security. He was caught up in the day-to-day activities of business ownership, so he

Deborah Read married Benjamin Franklin in 1730.

had little time for scientific studies. He did, however, continue to read and study, and he associated with other people who shared his interest in science.

By 1732, the *Pennsylvania Gazette* had become profitable, and Franklin had also obtained a financial interest in other gazettes in South Carolina and Rhode Island, yet he was still not satisfied. His goal was not just to earn more money; he also wanted to find some sort of creative outlet—perhaps even a new character to play, since Silence Dogood had been such a hit. His solution was to invent a new persona, Richard Saunders, and to create a book called *Poor Richard's Almanack.*

Franklin knew people loved almanacs—pocket-sized, paperback calendar books with calculations about the tides, changes in the moon, weather forecasts, and other information. Almanacs were so popular that nearly every household had one. *Poor Richard's Almanack* was similar to other almanacs because it was published annually and included much of the same information. What made *Poor Richard's* unique was its humorous writings, as well as "Richard's" words of wisdom. Sayings that appeared in the book, such as "Well done is better than well said," "A penny saved is a penny earned," "Never confuse motion with action," and "Haste makes waste" are still used today. *Poor Richard's* wisdom was also colored with a tinge of sarcasm, which was evident in sayings like "God heals and the doctor takes the fees," "Fish and visitors stink after three days," and "A country man between two lawyers is like a fish between two cats."

Poor Richard's Almanack was a huge success and it developed a loyal readership almost immediately. Franklin continued to write and publish it annually for the next 25 years, and its growing popularity and steady sales helped make him a wealthy man.

"Early to bed and early to rise, makes a man healthy, wealthy, and wise."

—BENJAMIN FRANKLIN, FROM *POOR RICHARD'S ALMANACK*

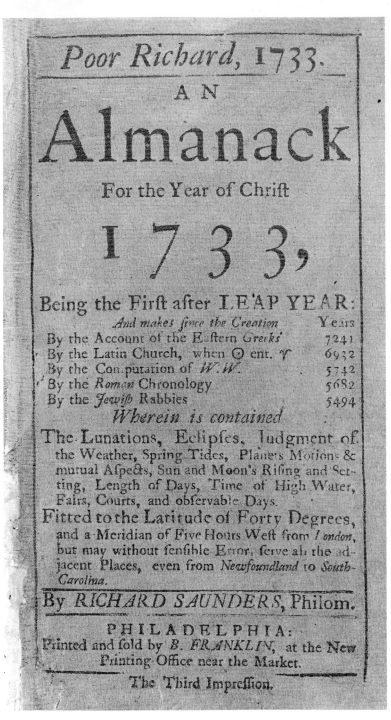

Poor Richard, 1733.

AN

Almanack

For the Year of Christ

1733,

Being the First after LEAP YEAR:

And makes since the Creation   Years

By the Account of the Eastern *Greeks*	7241
By the Latin Church, when ☉ ent. ♈	6932
By the Computation of *W.W.*	5742
By the *Roman* Chronology	5682
By the *Jewish* Rabbies	5494

Wherein is contained

The Lunations, Eclipses, Judgment of the Weather, Spring Tides, Planets Motions & mutual Aspects, Sun and Moon's Rising and Setting, Length of Days, Time of High Water, Fairs, Courts, and observable Days.

Fitted to the Latitude of Forty Degrees, and a Meridian of Five Hours West from *London*, but may without sensible Error, serve all the adjacent Places, even from *Newfoundland* to *South-Carolina.*

By *RICHARD SAUNDERS*, Philom.

PHILADELPHIA:

Printed and sold by *B. FRANKLIN*, at the New Printing-Office near the Market.

The Third Impression.

What made Poor Richard's Almanack *different was its wit and words of wisdom.*

Franklin and other Junto club members started the first circulating library in the colonies.

The First Public Library

Franklin's publications satisfied his passion for writing, which he enjoyed about as much as he enjoyed reading. Books had taught him almost everything he had learned throughout his life, so he knew how valuable they were. He wanted to find a way to make books more available to others.

Several years before, in 1727, he had founded the Junto, a club composed of young men who met regularly to discuss social, economic, scientific, political, and intellectual issues. In their spirited discussions, the men often came up with questions whose answers were found only in books. At that time, however, books were both scarce and expensive, so few people had access to a wide selection of them. Franklin thought of a solution to this problem: Club members could pool their resources, buy a collection of books, and create a library that Junto members and others in the community could use.

The group approved Franklin's idea, and in 1731 the men drew up the official papers for the Library Company of Philadelphia. Together, the members decided which books they would order, on topics such as advanced science and mathematics, journalism, poetry, and general interest subjects. They ordered the books from England the following spring, and six months later, the Library Company of Philadelphia officially opened. It was the first circulating library in America, and today, the organization nicknamed "the mother of all research libraries" still operates in Philadelphia.

Philadelphia's First Fire Department

The civic-mindedness that inspired Franklin to found the library also motivated him to think about Philadelphia's risk of fire. During his stay in London, he had been impressed with the city's elaborate fire protection system, which had been established after London's disastrous fire in 1666. Franklin became concerned that if a fire were to rage out of control in Philadelphia, the city was not prepared to fight it effectively.

In 1735, Franklin discussed his concerns with the Junto, and then wrote and printed a letter in his *Gazette* under the pen name of "A.A." In the letter, he warned of the dangers of fire, offered preventive measures for homeowners, and recommended that the city make a collective effort to be prepared. He also coined the famous phrase, "An ounce of prevention is worth a pound of cure" and mentioned that Boston had formed clubs of men whose specialty was to fight fires. He recommended this same preventive action for Philadelphia.

Franklin started a fire company after becoming acquainted with the fire protection Londoners instituted after the Great Fire of London of 1666.

The people in Philadelphia agreed with Franklin's idea, and organized the city's first "fire club" of 30 men. In 1736, under the guidance of Franklin and the Junto, the Union Fire Company was officially incorporated.

Franklin was proud of the fire club, and he considered it one of his greatest accomplishments. Yet, the year he formed the club was also one of the saddest years of his life. His son Francis, whom he had nicknamed "Franky," died of smallpox at the age of four.

Intellectual Pursuits

During the late 1730s and early 1740s, Franklin was well known in Philadelphia as a successful businessman and community leader. He was appointed as clerk of the Pennsylvania Assembly in 1736, and became Philadelphia's postmaster in 1737.

In 1743, Franklin had an idea for a new group that would be similar to the Junto, yet include men from colonies other than Pennsylvania. Modeled after one of the world's most distinguished scientific organizations, the Royal Society of London, the group would bring together "inquiring minds" and promote a better understanding of arts and science. Franklin wanted the men to share their collective knowledge about such scientific subjects as botany, medicine, archaeology, mathematics, chemistry, and physical geography.

Franklin formally organized his group and named it the American Philosophical Society. Members included a physician, a botanist, a mathematician, a chemist, and a geographer, and all were men who had a serious interest in science. Although Franklin was busy with his newspaper and community activities, his involvement in the society gave him an opportunity to consult with other intellectuals who were as serious about science as he was.

Observations in Nature

One of Franklin's interests was meteorology, and in 1743 he made a weather-related observation that earned him respect as one of the world's first meteorologists. One October evening, he planned to watch an eclipse of the moon, but he was unable to see it because the sky was obscured by the clouds of a northeasterly storm. He later read about the storm in a Boston newspaper and discovered

A lunar eclipse led Benjamin Franklin to change the common idea about storms.

that the storm did not arrive there until later in the evening, so people in Boston had been able to see the eclipse. The average person would not have thought twice about this, but Franklin was puzzled. He knew that Boston was 400 miles northeast of Philadelphia, and he would have expected a northeasterly storm to hit Boston first.

Over the next few weeks, he collected information from friends in Boston, and after he studied it, he came to a conclusion: The common belief about northeasterly storms was wrong—they did not travel in the same direction as the wind; they traveled in the opposite direction of the wind. These storms started with cold winds that originated in the northeast, and then pulled warmer air up from the southwest. Once the storms were formed, they traveled in a circular pattern, which explained why a storm would hit Philadelphia before Boston. This theory was unheard of in Franklin's time, but it later became the basis for meteorological knowledge about whirling wind systems known as cyclones.

Franklin often made this sort of astute observation because he constantly wanted to know why things happened in nature. Also, his curiosity was not limited to complex phenomena such as weather patterns; some of the simplest natural occurrences often caught his attention. Even something as small and seemingly insignificant as ants interested him.

Franklin had a strong hunch that ants had a way to communicate with each other, so he performed an experiment to find out if he was correct. After he discovered ants in a pot of molasses in his closet, he shook out all but one of the insects and hung the pot from a string attached to the ceiling. He observed that when the lone ant had eaten enough molasses, it traveled up the string to the ceiling, then made its way down the wall to the floor. Within 30 minutes, it was mobbed by a swarm of the other ants, as if they wanted to hear the news it had to tell about the molasses. The entire colony of ants then followed in reverse the same course that the lone ant had traveled—up the wall, across the ceiling, down the string, and into the pot. When they had eaten enough, they all followed the lone ant's same path back down to the floor. From this experiment, Franklin determined that as he had suspected, ants did indeed communicate with each other.

The same year that Franklin made his observations about northeasterly storms and ants, he and his wife had another child. Their daughter Sarah, whom Franklin nicknamed "Sally," was born in September 1743.

> "In any age, in any place, Franklin would have been great."
>
> — CARL VAN DOREN, BIOGRAPHER

The Franklin Stove

Franklin performed some experiments, such as those that involved seaweed and ants, merely to satisfy his own curiosity. There were others, though, that led him to invent better ways to do things. One example of this was his Pennsylvania fireplace, which was later named the Franklin stove.

Pennsylvania winters were often extremely cold, and Franklin had thought for years about the way people heated their homes. All houses had fireplaces, but they did not heat very well. They burned wood too quickly, which cost the homeowner more money for fuel, and they also allowed most of the heat to escape through the chimney.

Franklin designed and built a better fireplace. It was the first heating device made of iron, and it featured a number of passages and vents. The vents could draw cold air in from the outside, warm it in the air passages, and then circulate it throughout the room. The fireplace was designed to make heat stay in the room rather than escape up the chimney, and it had a damper that closed the chimney when the fireplace was not in use.

By the early 1740s, Franklin was satisfied with his design, and he contracted with a fellow Junto member to manufacture and sell the new fireplace. The invention became popular immediately, and as the weather became colder, more and more fireplaces sold.

The Franklin stove was made of iron. Its ability to heat an entire room made it a huge success.

When the governor of Pennsylvania heard about the invention, he was so pleased that he offered Franklin a patent, which would give him the exclusive right to sell it. Franklin declined the offer because he was not interested in patents or the financial benefits he could gain from his fireplace. He believed that his true reward was the satisfaction he got when he invented items that made his life—and the lives of others—easier and more productive.

Renewed Focus: Electricity

By 1748, Franklin had achieved professional success and had enough wealth to sustain his and his family's lifestyle, so he decided to retire. He still intended to remain involved with his newspaper and to continue the publication of *Poor Richard's Almanack*, but he wanted more time for his scientific interests.

The invention of the Leyden jar and the findings of European scientists intrigued him, and he wanted to explore the mysterious science of electricity for himself.

Franklin had read and studied enough to know that all matter contained some amount of electrical charge. After he built and experimented with a number of electrical apparatuses based on the Leyden jar, he was convinced that electricity was fluid in nature. He theorized that the amount of electrical fluid contained in matter could be measured on a scale that ranged from "positive" (an excessive amount of electrical fluid), to "neutral" (a normal amount of electrical fluid), to "negative" (a lesser amount of electrical fluid). He believed

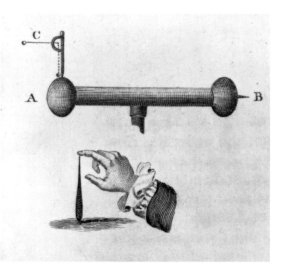

Franklin illustrated his idea for a lightning rod in his book Experiments and Observations on Electricity.

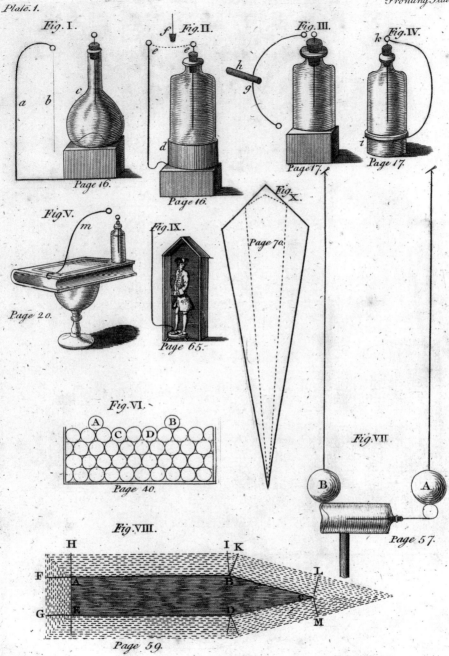

Franklin's experimentation with apparatuses based on the Leyden jar caused him to believe that electricity could be measured.

that depending on how much electrical fluid matter contained, the charges contained within it either attracted or repelled each other. During this process, electrical fluid was transferred from one body to the other, and no fluid was lost.

Based on his analysis of the Leyden jar, Franklin determined that the glass in which electricity was stored did not necessarily need to be a jar. So in 1749, he created the first "electrical battery," an apparatus made of 11 panes of window glass and lead plates, connected together with wire. Once he created an electrical charge, he believed, the battery could store electricity to be used later.

A Dangerous Experiment

Franklin tried this idea himself, in an electrical experiment that was especially foolhardy—in fact, he later referred to it as a "notorious blunder." Just before Christmas in 1750, he built a battery with six large glass jars, in which he had created a strong electrical charge. He then used the powerful force of the electricity to shock a live turkey. This created a blinding flash and a noise that sounded like a gunshot; and while it did kill the turkey, it also shot electricity through Franklin's body and sent him into seizures that almost killed him. He did say later, however, that the cooked turkey was uncommonly tender.

Lightning and Electricity

As he continued his experiments, Franklin became more curious not just about electricity, but about the similarities it shared with lightning. He recorded in a journal that both electricity and lightning gave off light and were the same color; both traveled swiftly and traveled in crooked paths; both could pass through metal and could even melt it; both made a loud "crack" or exploding noise when they made contact with an object; both had a sulphur-like smell; both could cause fires; and both could travel through water or ice. These similarities strengthened Franklin's belief that lightning was an electrical current in nature.

Opposite: *Franklin wrote in his journal that electricity and lightning had the similar qualities of giving off light and traveling in a crooked path.*

In the course of his experiments, Franklin had discovered that electricity was attracted to pointed objects, like pieces of wire. He was sure that this was true but he did not fully understand why, and it piqued his curiosity. It also deepened his desire to explore the connection between lightning and electricity: If they were the same, he believed it would be possible to protect houses, churches, and ships from lightning strikes. Franklin's idea was to construct something that was later termed a lightning rod: a pointed iron rod that could be erected on a structure, with a wire that led toward the ground (or the water in the case of a ship), that would divert lightning away from the structure itself.

In 1750, Franklin shared all his theories about electricity, as well as his beliefs about its connection with lighting, in a letter to his friend Peter Collinson, the Library Company's agent in London. Collinson, a man with wide scientific interests and influential connections, gave the letter to the publisher of London's *Gentleman's Magazine*. In 1751, the publisher printed Franklin's observations in a pamphlet entitled *Experiments and Observations on Electricity Made at Philadelphia in America*.

Once Franklin was convinced about the connection between electricity and lightning, he was determined to find a way to prove it. His original idea was to erect a lightning rod on a church steeple, but when the construction of the steeple was delayed, he was forced to devise another way to prove the connection. The result was his famous kite experiment.

Musical Lightning

Franklin liked to test his theories, even if he had to perform potentially deadly experiments. One daring experiment in 1752 involved a lightning rod that he constructed on his own house, which was designed to ring bells when an electrical current was present in the air.

To the top of his chimney he attached an iron rod with a wire fastened to the bottom. The wire ran through a covered glass tube in the roof and down through a staircase, where it was divided into two parts. He attached a bell to each end of the wire and suspended a brass ball on a silk thread between the two bells. Then he waited to see what would happen.

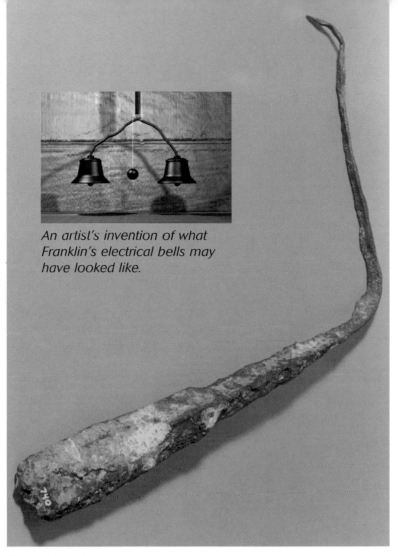

An artist's invention of what
Franklin's electrical bells may
have looked like.

Franklin's lightning rod.

Fortunately for Franklin, his invention did not attract a direct
lightning strike; if it had, his home would likely have gone up in
flames. What he did observe was that under certain weather con-
ditions, the bells rang, while at other times, electric arcs flashed
between the bells, and lit up the entire room with a stream of electricity that he likened to bright sunshine. He came to the conclusion that anytime there was electricity in the air, the bells would
ring. This eventually became annoying, and he disconnected his
musical electricity device.

Fame and Recognition

Throughout the course of his electrical studies, Franklin had published his findings in both the *Pennsylvania Gazette* and *Poor Richard's Almanack*. He also communicated regularly with Collinson, who shared excerpts of *Experiments and Observations on Electricity* with the Royal Society of London. In a letter, Collinson reported that Franklin had earned the Society's admiration for his intelligence, as well as the unique nature of his experiments.

Franklin's reputation as a brilliant scientist spread throughout the American colonies and Europe. Scientists everywhere began to consider him a master of electrical research. In 1753, Franklin received an honorary Master of Arts degree from Harvard College, followed by the same honor from two other distinguished colleges—Yale and the College of William and Mary. Also in 1753,

In 1753, Franklin was given an honorary Master of Arts degree from Harvard, the college Silence Dogood had criticized in the New England Courant.

Franklin received the coveted Sir Godfrey Copley gold medal from the Royal Society of London, and three years later he was elected as a member of that society. Before the end of the decade, he also received a Doctor of Laws degree from Scotland's St. Andrews University, and from that point on he was known as Dr. Franklin.

Franklin was honored to be recognized for his scientific accomplishments and was proud of his degrees and awards; still, his motivation had never been to become famous. He was a humble man, with working class roots. What motivated him most was the joy of discovery and the satisfaction he got when he unraveled the mysteries of nature.

"Your very curious pieces relating to electricity and thundergusts have been read before the Society and have been deservedly admired not only for the clear intelligent style but also for the novelty of the subjects."

— PETER COLLINSON, IN A LETTER TO FRANKLIN ON BEHALF OF THE ROYAL SOCIETY OF LONDON

The First Storm Chaser

Franklin's quest to understand nature had made him curious about weather and storms for many years. In 1755, he made a weather-related discovery that eventually won him the nickname, "The First Storm Chaser."

As he rode a horse through the Maryland countryside, Franklin spotted a small whirlwind that spun like a top and gained force as it moved from the valley up the side of a hill. By the time it got closer to him, the whirlwind had become 40 or 50 feet high and 20 to 30 feet in diameter, and it traveled along in a zigzag pattern, similar to a small tornado. A more cautious person might have been afraid, since this whirlwind could possibly be dangerous. Not only did Franklin continue to watch it, however, he took off on his horse and rode alongside it. He even struck at it with his whip to see if he could break it up. He followed it for three-quarters of a mile, and when the whirlwind starting to break off tree limbs and send them flying in his direction, he decided it was time to call off the chase. He later learned that the whirlwind was a form of "dust devil," a spinning wind made visible by the dust and debris it picked up as it grew larger.

The behavior of the dust devil strengthened Franklin's belief that weather systems moved over distances, and often changed as they traveled. Although those weather systems could not be altered or controlled (as he proved with his whip), their progress could be charted and predicted with some accuracy.

Franklin the Diplomat

It was around this time that Franklin began to spend more time on his political duties. Several years before, in 1751, he had been elected to the Pennsylvania Assembly, which meant that he represented Philadelphia in the legislature and helped make laws for the colony.

In the mid-1750s, the Assembly began to clash with one of Pennsylvania's most influential landowners, and with the state's governor, over equal taxation of property. The issues were serious and had to be presented to Parliament, so the assembly needed a representative who could speak on its behalf.

Franklin had lived for a while in London and was familiar with England and its people. He was highly regarded as a scientist and as a member of the Royal Society of London. He was also respected by the people in his own state, as well as throughout the colonies, for his dedication to "promoting the public good." For these reasons, in 1757 the Pennsylvania Assembly chose him to travel to England to act as its negotiator.

During his years in England, Franklin made progress in his negotiations on Pennsylvania's behalf. He also became an established figure in London society, someone who was known as one of the greatest thinkers on earth. He regularly attended meetings of the Royal Society, and associated with his friend Peter Collinson, as well as many other scholars, physicians, and scientists—people he described as "sensible, virtuous, and elegant minds." He often traveled between London and Paris, and was welcomed into the most elite social circles.

Forever the Inventor

As always, science was never far from Franklin's mind. He amazed people with his wide breadth of knowledge about diverse topics,

Franklin (seated) traveled to England as Pennsylvania's spokesman.

and he was at ease when he socialized with experts in fields such as electricity, meteorology, geology, and mathematics. He had already proven that even when he observed the simplest phenomena, he had to apply scientific principles to figure out how and why they occurred. It was this trait that led him to create yet another invention in 1761—this time, a musical instrument.

During Franklin's time, musicians who performed on musical glasses were popular throughout Europe. These simple instruments were made up of glasses that contained varying amounts of water. To play them, musicians rubbed their wet fingers around the glasses' brims. Franklin was charmed by the unique sound of the music—so much so that he was inspired to build an instrument that used the same principle, but without the water. He named it the "glass armonica," after the Italian word for "harmony."

He started with 37 glasses of varying sizes, and removed the stems. He drilled a hole in the bottom of each glass, put corks in

Franklin became an expert player of the glass armonica he invented in 1761.

the holes, and nested the glasses inside each other to make them more compact and easy to play. He then mounted the glasses on a horizontal spindle, which was connected to a foot pedal. As he pressed the pedal with his foot, the spindle turned and spun the glasses; when he touched a moistened finger to the edges of the glasses, the instrument produced a variety of musical tones that Franklin described as "incomparably sweet."

Franklin became an expert player of his glass armonica, and he frequently entertained guests with performances. Eventually, the instrument became so popular that even famous composers such as Mozart and Beethoven wrote songs to be played on it. In later years, craftsmen improved on Franklin's design and began to build modern versions of this unique musical instrument. Today, although glass armonicas are rare, they are still in existence.

Home Again

By the time Franklin invented his glass armonica, he had been in England for nearly five years and he thought he might be ready to return to Philadelphia. He had mixed feelings about whether he should leave the mother country—now that he had lived there for so long, he had made many friends, and he enjoyed his life there. He missed America, though, so he decided it was time to go home, and he returned to Philadelphia.

Troubled Times

Franklin arrived home with the belief that even though there were differences between England and the colonies, they could be set-tled peacefully. Although America remained under British rule, England left the colonies alone for the most part, and allowed local governments to do most of their own lawmaking.

By the early 1760s, however, tension had developed over issues of taxation and government, and the colonies' relationship with England became strained. Franklin, like most Americans, believed that "taxa-tion without representation" was wrong; in other words, if Americans were expected to pay taxes to England, then they should be repre-sented in Parliament, the British lawmaking body, so they would have a say in how those taxes were determined and how much they should be. The British did not agree.

In 1764, the Pennsylvania Assembly again chose Franklin to visit England as the state's spokesperson. While he was there, tension continued to grow in America and his role changed from the voice of Pennsylvania to the voice of the colonies.

This time, Franklin remained in England for more than ten years, and he worked to preserve the relationship between England and America. This was no easy task, and it required so much of his time that he had little time left to pursue science-related activities. England firmly believed that the colonies should respect British rule and should pay whatever taxes were levied on them. Americans, on the other hand, believed Parliament had no right to levy taxes without their representation and consent. As a diplomat, Franklin was caught in the middle of this heated debate. He believed that both sides had valid issues, and he wanted to help resolve those issues so England and the colonies could be at peace with each other.

The British government, which had incurred heavy debt from the French and Indian War, needed to find ways to collect revenue, and felt the answer was through taxation of the colonies. The first direct tax was the Stamp Act in 1765. Franklin argued against it and was instrumental in getting it repealed less than a year later. Parliament was not finished with its taxation efforts, however. It passed the Townshend Acts in 1768, which taxed almost everything the colonists bought, including tea. The Acts were repealed two years later, but the tax on tea remained. By this time, America had had enough.

Determined not to drink tea that had been taxed without their consent, the colonists refused to buy English tea. This caused a major financial problem for England, but the colonists did not stop there. In 1773, when three British tea ships docked in Boston, a mob of men stormed the ships one night, chopped open chests full of tea, and flung 90,000 pounds of it into the harbor. This revolt became known as the Boston Tea Party.

British rulers were outraged. They perceived this resistance as an inexcusable act of defiance and immediately passed a series of laws designed to punish resisters and limit the colonies' freedom. These laws, which the colonists labeled the Intolerable Acts, confirmed America's worst fears: The British government did not care if it

In 1773, angry citizens dumped 90,000 pounds of British tea into Boston Harbor. This became known as the Boston Tea Party.

achieved an amicable relationship with the colonies. Its only motive was to control them.

When Franklin heard about the Boston Tea Party, he lost virtually all hope that the differences between America and England could be resolved. The more England attempted to tighten its hold on the colonies with new taxes and laws, the more resistant Americans became, and the more they threatened to revolt. In spite of this, Franklin felt loyal to both England and the colonies and wished for peace more than anything else. Something happened in 1774, however, that destroyed his loyalty toward England.

The Final Blow

An acquaintance of Franklin's had delivered a collection of letters to him, six of which had been written by Thomas Hutchinson, the governor of Massachusetts. Franklin would not divulge who gave him the letters or who wrote them, but they urged Parliament to force Americans to accept taxation, and spoke out against independence for the colonies. Franklin was shocked at what he considered Hutchinson's treasonous behavior, and he sent the letters to Boston to be analyzed by some of his contacts there. Even though he had urged that the letters not be made public, without his knowledge, they made their way into the hands of Hutchinson's enemies, who published them in the newspapers.

Benjamin Franklin was called before the British government and was blamed for talking about the Hutchinson letters.

When the colonists became aware of what Hutchinson had written, they were furious. How could a fellow colonist betray America and support Parliament's efforts toward reduced liberties and continued taxation? The British government was outraged as well. Confidential documents had been made public—and they blamed Benjamin Franklin for it.

In 1774, Franklin was called before the British government and condemned for his actions. He was shocked and angry at this treatment, yet he remained silent during his trial. After he had served as a peacemaker and negotiator for so many years, and had remained loyal to England for his entire life, the British government had turned against him.

Franklin stayed in England for one more year to finish his business affairs, and then he left the country. This time, he believed he would never return again.

Ocean Studies

When Franklin left England in 1775, he was deeply troubled. During his last year there, he had

"Benjamin Franklin is one of those rare men with regard to whom it seems almost impertinent for an ordinary mortal to write or to speak, whether in praise or blame."

— SIR ESME HOWARD, FORMER BRITISH AMBASSADOR

received word that his wife, Deborah, had died of a stroke. He had not seen her for many years, and he was saddened by her death. Also, he blamed himself for the collapse of the relationship between England and America. He had, after all, been the chief negotiator between England and the colonies. Still, he knew he had done everything he could. More than ever before, he was now completely committed to the American cause: independence.

Despite his personal and political problems, Franklin was too much of a scientist to dwell on them during the entire ocean voyage. As he had done in his earlier travels, he took time to observe the world around him. He had long been curious about the Gulf Stream, a current that existed in large bodies of water such as the Atlantic Ocean. The Gulf Stream continuously mystified ship captains because it seemed to affect how fast they could travel: Ships that traveled from England to America arrived at their destinations much faster than those headed in the opposite direction, from America to England.

As Franklin's ship crossed the ocean, he could distinguish where the Gulf Stream was because it was a different color from the rest of the water. He also noticed that more seaweed grew within the stream than in the surrounding water, and that whales swam around it but not inside it. From these observations, he concluded that the Gulf Stream must be a current of water that was warmer than the rest of the ocean. To test his theory, he decided to take the ocean's temperature.

For one week, at various times throughout the day, Franklin lowered a thermometer into the ocean to gauge the water temperature. What he discovered amazed him: The temperature inside the stream was as much as 19 degrees warmer than the water around it. Franklin thought this was a valuable discovery that would help ship captains better chart their voyages between continents, and he used the information to develop the first known charts that showed the Gulf Stream's location in the ocean. It was not until ten years later, however, that he took the time to formally write down his conclusions and make them public.

The Gulf Stream seemed to affect how fast ships could travel.

Alarming Developments

In May 1775 Franklin's ship arrived in Philadelphia, and he was greeted with some shocking news: As he had traveled across the ocean, the American colonists had begun to make plans to resist the British. They had stockpiled weapons to prepare for a British attack, and when British soldiers attempted to arrest them for illegal possession of the weapons, a bloody battle had ensued at two small towns near Boston. To this day, it is not clear who fired the first shot, but the battles at Lexington and Concord marked the beginning of the American Revolution.

Liberty Is Declared

When Franklin had made his decision to return to America, his intent was to retire from public life. His fellow colonists had other ideas, however. After all, who understood England and Parliament better than Franklin? Who was more qualified to advise them as they prepared for

"Yes, we must indeed all hang together, or most assuredly we shall all hang separately."
—BENJAMIN FRANKLIN

war and independence? Within 24 hours of Franklin's arrival in Philadelphia, the Pennsylvania Assembly elected him as a delegate to the newly formed Continental Congress, a patriotic group that had been formed to make plans for America's independence.

For the next year, he devoted his time and energy to the American cause. As a member of Congress, he was part of a committee that drafted the Declaration of Independence—a document that explained the colonies' break from England. On July 4, 1776, the Continental Congress approved the document; Benjamin Franklin, as well as all the other delegates, made it official when they added their signatures one month later.

The Declaration of Independence was a crucial first step, but it did not guarantee the colonies' independence. The war that had begun at Lexington and Concord still had to be fought, and the colonists knew that England was a formidable opponent, with the most powerful military force in the world. The Americans desperately needed help, and Congress decided that their best hope was France.

Another Long Journey

The colonies needed a representative who could visit France and convince the French government to help America in the war against England. Franklin was the obvious choice. He had achieved fame and respect throughout the world, and he had visited France many times during his years in England. He was also an experienced diplomat and a skilled negotiator. For all these reasons, Congress selected him to represent American interests in Paris.

By this time, Franklin was no longer a young man. He was 70 years old and his health was in decline. Even so, his intellect was as sharp as ever, and he was determined to do everything possible to help his country achieve independence. He also knew that he was the best person available for the job. He dreaded the long ocean voyage, but he gladly accepted the responsibility.

Life in France

In December 1776, Franklin sailed for Europe once again. When he arrived in Paris, he received a warm welcome and felt at home almost immediately. His reputation had preceded him; he was called "the celebrated Franklin," and "the man who had tamed lightning." The French people held him in high esteem for his vast scientific knowledge, especially his electrical discoveries. Franklin was a true American celebrity, and he was treated like one.

It took him just over a year to accomplish the goal he had been sent to achieve. In 1778, representatives from France and America signed two agreements: a treaty of amity and commerce, which guaranteed trade between America and France; and a treaty of alliance, which pledged French financial and military support for American independence. The war continued, but America was no longer in it alone.

Franklin remained in France, where he lived in the town of Passy, a suburb of Paris. After the Americans achieved victory in the Revolution, he spent much of his time at work with French and

---

Opposite: *Benjamin Franklin (seated, left), helped to draft the Declaration of Independence with John Adams (seated, center) and Thomas Jefferson (standing).*

This chromolithograph from 1882 shows Franklin being greeted warmly, and as a celebrity, by Parisians in 1776.

British officials to negotiate a formal peace treaty to end the war. Finally, in 1783, the Treaty of Paris was signed and formalized England's acceptance of the United States as an independent nation.

Now that the war was over, Franklin had more time to spend on his writing. During his last year and a half in France, he wrote a great deal, and much of his writing focused on matters of science.

A Practical Idea Begins as a Joke

One of Franklin's scientific ideas evolved out of something he had originally intended to be humorous. In a joking 1784 letter to the Parisian newspaper *Journal de Paris*, he noted that he had been accidentally awakened at the early hour of 6 o'clock in the morning and was surprised to see the sun shining brightly. He concluded that since French people typically slept until noon, they wasted valuable hours of daylight; thus, they should get up earlier in the day. By doing this, they would avoid using excessive amounts of candles to create "artificial daylight" during the evening hours.

Parisians scoffed at this advice, and they were put off by the notion that they should arise in the early hours of the morning. Decades later, however, Franklin's idea was put into action when clocks began to be turned one hour ahead in the spring. Today, daylight savings time is a reminder of Franklin's practical scientific wisdom.

An Ingenious Solution

Franklin was now in his late seventies. His eyesight, like that of most people his age, had deteriorated, so he needed two different sets of eyeglasses—one to help him read and write, and one to help him see from a distance. Franklin found it annoying to switch his glasses constantly, so he figured out a way to solve the problem. He took two pairs of glasses to an optician, and directed him to cut the lenses in half horizontally and fit the half-lenses into one frame, with the farsighted halves on top and the nearsighted halves on the bottom. Thanks to his "double spectacles," Franklin no longer had to change his glasses; instead, he just moved his eyes up when he wanted to see far away, and down when he wanted to see up close. His invention would one day be named "bifocals," and would help millions of people who had the same vision problem.

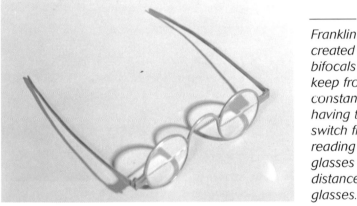

Franklin created bifocals to keep from constantly having to switch from reading glasses and distance glasses.

Welcome News

Franklin had lived in France for eight years, and he wanted to return to America. He had enjoyed his life there, but he missed his own country. In May 1785, he finally received the message he had longed for: Congress had granted him permission to go home.

Franklin's many friends and colleagues in France begged him not to leave. He was almost 80 years old, however, and he knew he probably did not have many years left to live. He wanted to spend his final years in America, the place where he had been born and where his family lived.

A Productive Voyage

Franklin worried that he might not survive the long ocean voyage home, but the trip actually seemed to rejuvenate him. As he had often done before, he made scientific observations and wrote about them. He resumed his measurements of the Gulf Stream's temperature, and concluded that it was a "river of warm water" that flowed from south to north, over the colder water of the ocean. He believed that ship navigators would benefit if they used thermometers to determine where the Gulf Stream was. Those who sailed north should follow the stream of warm water, because they would travel along with the fast-moving current. Those who traveled south should avoid the Gulf Stream because it would slow them down.

"I enjoy, through mercy, a tolerable share of health. I read a great deal, ride a little, do a little business for myself, now and then for others, retire when I can, and go into company when I please; so the years roll round, and the last will come, when I would rather have it said 'He lived usefully' than 'He died rich.'"

—BENJAMIN FRANKLIN, IN A 1750 LETTER TO HIS MOTHER

Franklin recorded his scientific conclusions in a document called "Maritime Observations." He presented not only his findings about the Gulf Stream, but also his recommendations for safer ocean travel. These recommendations included the use of watertight compartments in ships to prevent sinking; ways to prevent damage from fire, lightning, or collision with ships or icebergs; management of lifeboats to allow escape from shipwrecks; and measures that passengers should take to help protect themselves while they traveled. This document distinguished Franklin as one of the first known experts in the field of oceanography.

He also wrote another document entitled "Description of a New Stove for Burning of Pitcoal, and Consuming All Its Smoke," which was based on a stove he had devised years before while he lived in London. Similar to his Pennsylvania fireplace, this stove burned coal instead of wood and was designed to consume all its own smoke. He recorded more of his ideas about fireplaces and proper ventilation in another document called "On the Causes and Cure of Smoky Chimneys."

This voyage back to America from France was more productive for Franklin than any of his other travels. In fact, during this time at sea, he wrote more about scientific matters than at any other time in his life.

Franklin Makes History

When Franklin arrived in Philadelphia, he was treated like the world's most famous celebrity. Hundreds of admirers greeted him at the wharf, and as he walked down the street, bells rang and cannons boomed in his honor. This spirit of celebration continued for over a week, and people often visited him to offer their congratulations and gratitude for his contribution toward America's freedom.

Once again, Franklin assumed that he would retire—and once again, his colleagues had other ideas for him. American leaders intended to create a political system for the United States, and they wanted to develop a formal written constitution that would serve as the legal framework for the new country. This document would be the supreme law of the land—the basis for all laws that were passed. Franklin could not resist the opportunity to become involved.

In July 1787, through the work of delegates from 12 of the 13 states who attended a meeting called the Constitutional Convention, a draft was complete. Franklin, who was not completely comfortable with the document's wording, still pleaded with all the delegates to sign it in the name of unity.

On September 17, 1787, the Constitution of the United States was signed. Benjamin Franklin, at 81 years of age, was the oldest delegate to sign it.

The World Loses a Great Man

Over the next few years, Franklin continued to write letters and visit with his friends, but his health failed rapidly. Yet even though he was confined to his bed, his scientific mind was at work. When a friend wrote to say that he had hearing problems, Franklin told of an experiment that he himself had tried. When he used his fingers to enlarge the openings in his ears, Franklin could hear his watch tick from halfway across the room. He suggested that his friend also try this technique.

One of Franklin's last writings exemplified his feelings about the country he had served for his entire life. In a letter to George Washington, the first president of the United States, Franklin wrote that he had expected to die much sooner but that he was happy he had lived long enough to see his country's new freedom become a reality.

Benjamin Franklin died quietly at his Philadelphia home on April 17, 1790, three months after his 84th birthday. His funeral was the largest that had ever been held in America, with an estimated 20,000 people in attendance. He was buried in the Christ Church burial ground in Philadelphia, next to his wife Deborah.

Benjamin Franklin's death was a loss not only for America, but for the entire world. He had made amazing contributions to the areas of science, philosophy, and politics. He was a patriot and a diplomat, as well as a brilliant scientist—someone who was known for his genius, but who always believed that the true value of knowledge was not the knowledge itself, but its benefit to humanity. Because of all he accomplished, and everything he gave to the world, his legacy lives on today.

Benjamin Franklin was buried in Philadelphia, next to his wife Deborah.

IMPORTANT DATES

1706	Benjamin Franklin is born in Boston, Massachusetts
1716	Goes to work for his father, Josiah Franklin, after attending school for less than two years
1718	Begins work as printer's helper for his brother, James Franklin
1723	Runs away from Boston for New York, then moves to Philadelphia
1724	Leaves for England to buy equipment for new business; is stranded and is forced to find a job in London; stays for 18 months, then returns to America
1727	Forms the Junto in Philadelphia
1729	Becomes the owner of the *Philadelphia Gazette*
1730	Marries Deborah Read in a common law ceremony in Philadelphia
1731	Establishes the first circulating library in America; son William is born
1732	Writes and publishes first edition of *Poor Richard's Almanack*, which he continues to publish for the next 25 years; son Francis is born
1736	Founds the Union Fire Company, the first "fire club" in Philadelphia; appointed Clerk of the Pennsylvania Assembly; son Francis dies of smallpox
1743	Daughter Sarah is born
1748	Retires from printing business to focus on studies and experiments in electricity
1750	Writes *Experiments and Observations in Electricity*, which is published in London in 1751
1751	Elected as representative to the Pennsylvania Assembly
1752	Famous kite experiment proves lightning's connection with electricity
1753	Receives honorary degrees from Harvard College, Yale, and the College of William and Mary; also receives Copley gold medal from the Royal Society of London
1757	Travels to England in an attempt to reconcile differences between England and the colonies; remains there for five years
1759	Receives Doctor of Laws degree from University of St. Andrews in Scotland
1764	Returns to England in the hope of salvaging relations between America and Great Britain; lives there for over ten years
1774	Condemned by British government for releasing confidential Hutchinson letters to the public; his wife, Deborah, dies and is buried in Philadelphia
1775	Leaves England for the last time; resolves to work for American independence
1776	Helps draft and signs Declaration of Independence
1776	Travels to France to enlist aid for the American Revolution
1778	Successfully negotiates treaties with France that guarantee financial and military support for America's war with England

IMPORTANT DATES

1783 Peace treaty signed with England that establishes United States of America as independent country, and officially ends the war

1785 Leaves France to return to America; writes "Maritime Observations" and other scientific papers during voyage

1787 Oldest delegate at Constitutional Convention; encourages all delegates to sign it in the name of American unity; signs the United States Constitution

1790 Dies at age 84 and is buried in Philadelphia

GLOSSARY

Battery: A group of electric cells that, when combined, form an electric current

Condenser: A device that has the ability to store electrical energy

Conductor: Any material that allows electricity to pass through it

Electric shock: A sudden discharge of electricity from a charged object

Electrical current: A continuing flow of electrically charged particles

Electricity: A natural phenomenon that consists of negative and positive charges, observable in the attractions and repulsions of various forms of matter

Electrify: To charge with electricity

Friction: The natural heat caused when one object is rubbed against another

Lightning rod: A metal rod that is set up on a structure to protect it from lightning

Meteorology: The science of weather

Oceanography: A science that deals with the study of oceans

Resin: A natural organic substance, such as tar or amber

Science: Knowledge gained through experience or observations; proof, as opposed to assumption

FOR MORE INFORMATION

BOOKS

Beverley Birch, *Benjamin Franklin's Adventures With Electricity*. Hauppauge, N.Y.: Barron's, 1995. A book about scientific exploration that discusses Franklin's brilliance, and tells how his many electrical experiments led the way toward future explorations in electricity.

H.W. Brands, *The First American: The Life and Times of Benjamin Franklin*. New York: Doubleday, Division of Random House, Inc., 2000. A meticulously researched and comprehensive biography of Benjamin Franklin.

Lisa Jo Rudy, *The Ben Franklin Book of Easy and Incredible Experiments*. New York: John Wiley & Sons, 1995. Includes some biographical information about Franklin, and five chapters of hands-on scientific activities and experiments that cover some of his major interests: weather, electricity, music, paper and printing, light, and sound.

Esmond Wright, *Benjamin Franklin: His Life As He Wrote It*. Cambridge, Mass.: Harvard University Press, 1996. An updated edition of Franklin's autobiography that includes letters, notes, essays, diary entries, speeches, interviews, and articles. Extends beyond 1758, where Franklin's original autobiography ends.

WEB SITES

The Electric Ben Franklin

A USHistory.org site that includes a wealth of information about Benjamin Franklin such as details of his kite experiment, a collection of articles, and a complete online reproduction of Franklin's autobiography. http://www.ushistory.org/franklin/index.htm

The Franklin Institute Online

A site by the Franklin Institute Science Museum. One of the most valuable aspects is the site's searchable database, which allows access to research on astronomy, aviation, biology, earth science, physics, history, and many other topics. http://sln.fi.edu

The Writings of Benjamin Franklin

Contains the actual texts written by Franklin, including all 14 of his "Silence Dogood" letters, and many more of his writings. http://www.historycarper.com/resources/twobf1/contents.htm

INDEX